Grandpa's White Cane

Written by
Jim Hoxie and Joanna Jones

Illustrated by
Alex Portal

Chicken Creek Communications

Special thanks to:
Mountain Valley Vision Center, Creekside Elementary School, and Fort Meade VA Hospital.

Page 15 Bulletin Board represents the many commanders of the American Legion and the Veteran of Foreign Wars. On the left column are the caps for American Legion post 33, including (from top to bottom) the Commander, Vice Commander, Past Commander, and PUFL officer. On the right column are caps for the Veterans of Foreign Wars post 2730 (from top to bottom) Commander VFW 2730; District 10 Past Commander, 1962-63, Sturgis, South Dakota; Life Member VFW 2730; Grand Commander for South Dakota 1967-68.

Library of Congress Cataloging-in-Publication Data
Names: Hoxie, Jim and Joanna Jones, authors.
Title: Grandpa's White Cane
Description: Chicken Creek Communications, LLC,
Rapid City, SD, 2020.
Identifiers: Library of Congress Control Number: 2020919521 |
ISBN 978-0-9973849-6-3 (hardcover) |
Subjects: Author: Hoxie, Jim | Subject: Hoxie, Jim | Subject: Canes for the blind – Juvenile literature. | Subject: Blind – Rehabilitation – United States – Juvenile literature. | Subject: Veterans Administration Hospital (Hines, Ill.) – Juvenile literature. | Subject: United States – Veterans Health Administration – Blind Rehabilitation Service – Juvenile literature. | Subject: Visually impaired persons – Veterans. | Subject: People with visual disabilities -- United States -- Biography -- Juvenile literature.
Classification: LCC HV1593 | DDC 362.4 Hox – dc23
Summary: When Grandpa loses his sight, he attends a school for veterans who are visually impaired. There he regains his confidence for independent living. Grandpa shares these experiences and talks about educating children about the tall white cane.

Grandpa, tell me again why you use a white cane.

Well, I didn't always have a white cane. When I was your age, I went to school just like you. I learned to read, write, and do math.

Encourage the person to be involved in activities.

When I was in high school, I played football and learned to drive a car. Before I left home, my mother taught me how to cook and do my own laundry.

Then I went into the United States Army where I was a Military Policeman. After my military service I attended college and studied forestry to learn a lot about trees. My job with the lumber mill was to work in the forest marking trees that needed to be cut by lumberjacks.

Tell your friends what white canes mean.

During this time, Grandma and I raised our children. But when grandchildren began to enter our family, my eyes began to fail me.

My vision blurred and I could see halos around lights. After three minutes of reading, my eyes watered too much for me to continue, and I began to have severe headaches. The optometrist, eye doctor, diagnosed my eyes with a disease called glaucoma.

Despite a lot of medical procedures and taking eye medications, my vision kept decreasing. That is when I began to really think about the possibility of going blind and how my life would change. I knew I wanted to stay safe and yet be independent as I moved around doing my regular daily activities.

Offer your elbow for guidance.

I tried to use a regular cane to help me feel curbs and obstacles in my way. But as my vision continued to be more blurred, I needed more light to see. The doctor suggested that I use a tall white cane, so I purchased a tall white cane with a red tip. With this cane I could avoid obstacles, find steps, identify curbs, and get through doorways easier than before.

To get used to walking with my tall white cane, on nice days I walked with my friends along the path by the creek near my house. Walking with a human guide allowed me to enjoy my time outside. I could smell the flowers and fresh mown grass. Even the air was rich with moisture and I could hear the rushing water cascade over the rocks. I could not clearly see the creek anymore, but I could remember the beauty around me.

Take time to be a friend.

If my friends and I walked by a street, I could hear cars going by. Their speed startled me and I was concerned because I couldn't see them as they approached. I was thankful for my friends who wanted to help me be independent. Along the sidewalk, people were polite to step aside while we passed. Drivers stopped their cars while we crossed the road. Walking with a human guide helped me cross the street safely.

But I wanted to go by myself. I wanted to get more exercise and spend more time outdoors. I didn't want to rely on my friends, so I had to try it alone.

**Allow
the person
to speak
for himself.**

First I tried being independent in my garden. In my small twenty feet by thirty feet plot, I made wide rows for me to walk among the plants. I turned over dirt for planting. I grew radishes, beans, peas, corn, lettuce, tomatoes and zucchini. But when I was weeding, I had to get very close to the plants to be sure I was pulling weeds and not the plants I wanted to keep. Success! I could do the gardening.

Then I tried to do my woodworking projects. I sanded regular canes I had promised friends. I varnished and painted wood as I needed it. I realized I did not always feel safe using some of the big power tools. Sometimes I would have to rely on my friends to help me with the major cuts on the boards. Still, I felt I was being independent, and being visually impaired, I wanted to be as independent as possible.

Ask the person if he wants help.

Next, I tried walking alone with my tall white cane along the creek. The first few times, I did okay. But sometimes people were not very polite. One day unexpectedly, a lady's dog jumped up on me. I had not even seen the dog that was with her. She had not controlled her dog. While she was saying, "I'm so sorry," I wondered what I could do to protect myself from the next dog.

Another time a boy on a bicycle raced by me and I stepped away and off the path. I was stumbling and could have easily fallen if the ground had been uneven. Now I strained to hear everything around me. I felt very concerned for my safety.

I would stop at a corner and look both ways, but what good was three feet of blurred vision? Standing at the curb, I listened and listened again for the sound of cars. One time I took two steps into the street and suddenly heard a car speeding towards me. I just froze in place hoping to not get hit. Then suddenly I stepped back and became off balanced. If I hadn't pulled my cane back, the car might have hit my cane.

Was I using the white cane properly? Maybe going to a school to receive instruction would help me feel safe and protected. Some people must not know that the white cane with a red tip means the person is visually impaired.

Give simple verbal directions.

Back at home, I decided I needed more help with the task of learning to be independent with a white cane. I had a county health nurse look up resources for me. She informed me that the Veterans Administration (VA) had a school for the visually impaired. I applied immediately.

Once accepted into the school, I left Grandma at home and flew to a suburb of Chicago, to attend the Central Blind Rehabilitation Center, Edward Hines Jr. VA Hospital, for six weeks. Their mission is to restore independence and quality of life for Veterans with visual impairment. Back at home my continued support and training would be at the VA Medical Center, Ft. Meade, SD.

While the Hines school was very informative, it was a great deal of work. Our days started with class sessions beginning at 7:45 in the morning and ending seven classes later at 3:45 in the afternoon. Each student had a personalized program of study and lived at the school in a private room with a full bath, satellite TV, DVD player, phone, talking book player, and radio. We received training in orientation and mobility with a white cane, relearned how to do activities of daily living and communication, had visual skills training, and manual skills training for hobbies and household repair.

Every day I practiced walking with my tall white cane. I walked in the building, between the campus buildings, and even went shopping. The more I practiced sweeping and tapping the pathway before me, the more natural my walking became in crowded areas, across the streets, and up and down stairs.

Return items to their proper place.

I learned how blind people cook and I used my microwave a lot. To prepare my own breakfast was easy: wash your hands, get out the cereal from the same place, get out the bowl and spoon from their same places, and get out the milk from the same place in the refrigerator. Put your finger into the bowl and pour the cereal in until your finger can feel it. Then do the same with the milk.

I learned how to do my own laundry and how to separate clothes so colors matched when I wore them. It is hard to select clothes with very little vision. In my closet I put the colors together and keep them in the same place. A set of knots in the tag area indicate the colors. I could also use a digital reader, video call a friend, or ask Grandma to verify the colors.

With proper training I was able to use some power tools to make bird houses. Digital technologies were helpful to tell the time or read a book. I could fold money so I could identify the dollar amounts. The MOST important thing I learned was how to use the tall white cane correctly.

Now I felt comfortable to cross the street. I still could not see the traffic, but I knew how to listen to oncoming traffic and use the tall white cane.

Tell the person your name.

During the last week of my blind rehabilitation training, Grandma had to attend classes. She was learning how to make our home safe for me as well as letting me continue to independently do those things I had learned in my classes. We now knew how important it was to be organized, have a place for everything, and keep everything in its place.

When I came home, I wanted everyone to know more about tall white canes. I talked with my friends and that's when a couple of retired teachers asked me to share my story with the third grade students in our town.

What a great way for me to help students learn about how white canes are used in our society. I wanted to share the bigger issues associated with being visually impaired.

Keep pathways clear of objects.

The children needed to know that I grew up as a seeing person. When my eye disease glaucoma progressed, I had to start using a cane. The things I used at home on a daily basis had to stay in the same place for me to find them. The same place for my cereal, bowl, milk, spoon, and napkins. The same place for my toothpaste and toothbrush, my wallet, glasses and chairs. Any changes made my life more difficult.

During the classroom presentation, every child wanted to try to navigate around the student desks with a white cane. I had made a white cane for each student to use for the exercise. The students followed me using their white canes while briefly closing their eyes. This helped them to understand how Grandpa was seeing the world. The students would tap away, sweeping their own white canes left and right to hear the ping from hitting the legs of the metal desks. A more hollow sound let students know they found the trash can. Silent taps followed by clacking taps meant they had walked off the carpet and onto the tile portion of the floor.

Say "Passing on your left."

The students enjoyed stepping into my world for just a little while. Their thank yous came the next time they saw me on the path by the creek. As they rode their bicycles by me, they would ring their bicycle bells and holler out, "Hi! I'm on your left." That's just what we practiced in the classroom. I was so thankful and would tell them, "Oh, thank you." It feels so good to know that I am helping them understand about people who use white canes.

Since my training on how to use a tall white cane, I now can cross streets safely. I am no longer scared. I walk by myself a couple miles a day. It helps me to be physically fit and to be independent.

As I walk along the path by the creek, I enjoy the wonderful smells of nature.

Encourage confidence and independence in all daily activities.

Grandpa, are you ever going to get a Seeing Eye dog?

I don't know. Right now, my tall white cane and I do well together, but maybe someday.

Celebrate White Cane Safety Day – October 15

History of White Canes and White Cane Safety Day

Around the world, white canes are used by blind and visually impaired people to guide themselves in their travels. In 1921, James Briggs of Bristol, England, used a white cane to let pedestrians and vehicle traffic know he was blind. He chose to paint his cane white so it would be visible even at night. About ten years later, his cane design was standardized by Guilly d'Herbemont of France when 5,000 white canes were sent to blind French citizens and veterans from the First World War.

In the United States, George Bonham observed a blind man using a black cane. Bonham proposed painting the cane white with a red stripe to make it more noticeable. The first white cane laws were passed in 1930 in Bonham's hometown of Peoria, Illinois. Today, every state has a White Cane Law. It is estimated that 109,000 of the 1.3 million legally blind people in the United States use a white cane.

In the 1940s blind veterans returning home from the Second World War received white canes. In 1944, Richard E. Hoover, a veteran rehabilitation specialist, established the "Hoover Method," a technique of holding a long cane in the center of the body and swinging it back and forth before each step to detect obstacles. Today, this technique is called sweeping.

In 1963, the National Federation of the Blind sought to have White Cane Safety Day proclaimed as recognition of the rights of blind and visually impaired persons. Congress on October 6, 1964, authorized President Johnson to proclaim October 15 as White Cane Safety Day. The Lions Club International celebrates White Cane Day as Sight Conservation Day.

Dos and Don'ts for People with White Canes

A blind or visually impaired person is capable of doing many things; be sure to share daily activities together. The following list (in part) is from the Central Blind Rehabilitation Center, Edward Hines Jr. VA Hospital.

DO: Tell the person your name when you start talking with him.

DO: Tell the person you have extended your hand if you want to shake hands.

DO: Ask the person if they need help and how you can assist him.

DO: Encourage a visually impaired person to be as independent as possible.

DO: Encourage the person to socialize and engage in a wide variety of activities.

DO: Allow the blind person to speak for himself; don't do the talking for him.

DO: Educate friends and family about visual impairment and blindness.

DO: Give simple verbal directions; avoid pointing to a place or saying "over there."

DO: Try to give good visual descriptions of scenery, situations or events.

DON'T: Be overprotective or treat the blind person with pity.

DON'T: Avoid words such as "look" and "see" since they are words that are part of our everyday conversation.

DON'T: Leave a person without letting them know you are leaving.

DON'T: Forget to put things back where you found them, and don't rearrange things without discussing it first.

DON'T: Take over when a blind person is trying to do something; give them space to do it on their own.

DON'T: Allow others to speak to the blind person through you. Suggest, "You can ask him yourself." Or say, "He's right here, talk with him."

White Cane Information

Levels of blindness:

- **Visually impaired** people have a decreased ability to see. Their sight problems are not corrected by usual means, such as glasses. They have a little very blurred vision.

- **Totally blind** people have no vision. This would mean it is like going outside at night with your eyes closed.

Types of canes used by visually impaired and blind people:

- **White cane with a red tip** typically means that a person has low vision, is visually impaired, or otherwise has some usable eyesight.

- **Tall white canes** provide the most protection to a blind traveler who uses the cane to identify what lies ahead in the walk path. Some items the cane will help the user to detect are drop-offs, stairs, objects, grass lines, walls and openings.

- **Identification canes** (ID) are often lighter and shorter than the tall cane and not used as a mobility tool. The ID cane is only used to alert others of the user's visual impairment.

- **Support canes** are white canes with red tips usually about waist high and provide a similar function as the identification canes. Support canes identify a person as visually impaired, give some information about the environment, and aid with balance and physical stability.

Orientation and mobility using a tall white cane:

- **Sweeping** – The cane is moved back and forth to check the area in front of the walker to determine if the path is clear.

- **Ready to Cross** – The arm with the cane is extended out at waist height at a 45 degree angle. This position shows that the visually impaired person is ready to cross the street. The White Cane Traffic Law requires vehicle drivers to stop for any pedestrian carrying a white cane regardless of whether or not they are in a crosswalk.

- **Tapping** – The cane is used to touch an object on or near the ground to determine what it is, for example a trash can, a metal bench, or a brick wall.

Glossary

Certified Blind Rehabilitation Specialists – Instructors who are highly trained experts specialized in working with individuals who are blind or visually impaired. These instructors guide and empower their students to achieve their life goals. The use of assistive technology becomes daily support tools, such as specialized optical and electronic devices that enlarge images for viewing, speech-output computers and peripherals, global positioning devices, talking books, talking watches, auditory players, and money readers.

Certified Orientation and Mobility Specialists – Instructors for sequential processes in which visually impaired individuals are taught to utilize their remaining senses to determine their position within their environment and to negotiate safe movement from one place to another.

Glaucoma – A disease of the eye in which there is increased pressure within the eyeball, causing gradual loss of sight.

Human guide – A visually impaired person uses another person to lead or guide the way. It is called walking with a human guide.

20/20 vision – The standard or how a "normal" person sees. This 20 means: when you stand 20 feet away from an eye chart you can see what the normal person should see.

20/200 vision – A legally blind person with a vision of 20/200 has to be as close as 20 feet to identify objects that people with normal vision can spot from 200 feet away.

Legally blind – 20/200 vision or worse in the better seeing eye, or visual field of 20 degrees or less. Two leading causes for blindness are macular degeneration and diabetes.

Low vision – 20/70 to 20/200 vision in the better seeing eye, may also include central or peripheral field loss.

Ophthalmologist – A medical doctor who can perform medical and surgical interventions for eye conditions. The doctor provides vision services.

Optometrist – A person licensed to conduct eye exams, prescribe corrective contact lenses and glasses, and diagnose and treat eye diseases. The person has a doctor of optometry degree.

References

Pearson, Jaci Conrad (August 29, 2018). Rocket bat box a retirement gift between two kindred spirits. *Black Hills Pioneer Newspaper*, Spearfish, SD.

Portal, Alex. (October 12, 2018). White cane safety day: Spearfish man shares his personal story of blindness. *Black Hills Pioneer Newspaper*, Spearfish, SD.

Vornholt, Jerry. (2019). *Legacy of the overcomers: Character validation*. A new vision, pp. 17-26. Peppertree Press, Sarasota, FL.

Sources

The following organizations provide information and services to anyone who is interested in knowing more information about blind and visually impaired people.

- American Council of the Blind (800) 424-8666
- American Foundation for the Blind (800) 232-5463
- Central Blind Rehabilitation Center, Edward Hines Jr. VA Hospital, Blind Rehabilitation Family Education (708) 202-2272
- National Federation of the Blind (410) 659-9314
- Light House for the Blind and Visually Impaired (415) 431-1481

Resources available in each state are dependent upon the state. Funding for the visually impaired and blind is allocated in the state budget. Some of South Dakota state resources are:

- South Dakota Department of Human Services: Services to the Blind and Visually Impaired (800) 265-9684
- South Dakota School for the Blind and Visually Impaired (888-275-3814)
- South Dakota Association of the Blind (SDAB) Sioux Falls, SD (605) 941-9512
- National Federation of the Blind (NFB) Rapid City, SD (605) 721-3311

Meet the Authors and Illustrator

Jim Hoxie worked as a professional forester and loves the outdoors. He spent many years hunting and fishing; now he devotes his time to gardening and woodworking.

Joanna Jones taught school for many years and now enjoys reading and sharing books with children and friends.

Alex Portal is a cartoonist, news reporter, and illustrator. He delights in watching stories come to life through his pictures.